I'd Rather Kiss A Goat

Dr. James L. Snyder

Fellowship Ministries
P.O. Box 831313 – Ocala. FL 34483
© 2023 BY FELLOWSHIP MINISTRIES

ALL RIGHTS RESERVED

Unless Otherwise Noted, Scripture Quotations Are From The Authorized (King James) Version of The Bible.

WEBSITES
www.whatafellowship.com
www.jamessnyderministries.com

ISBN: 9798866067732

Family of God Fellowship
PO Box 831313 – Ocala, FL 34483
jamessnyder51@Gmail.com
(352) 216-3025

Table of Contents

Introduction 5
Where Is The Gracious Mistress Of The Parsonage? 7
I Screamed For Ice Cream And Got In Trouble 11
What Would My Life Be Without A Cookie 15
Sow A Thought Reap A Pie 19
Ugly Isn't For Sissies 23
Another Celebration In The Bank 27
If I'm Not Crazy Nobody Is 31
Who's Been Fiddling With My Mind? 35
Nothing Like A Mystery To Calm My Nerves 39
Learning What "me-time" Is All About 43
I'm So Poor I Can't Pay Attention 47
What A Wacky World We Live In 51
Has Anyone Seen My Marbles? 55
The Princess Hath Thus Spoken 59
My Reward I'll Eat It If I Want To 63
I'd Rather Kiss A Goat 67
Dizzy Is As Dizzy Says 71
If Only I Had It My Way 75
Have Giggle Will Laugh 79
Oh, Memory, How I Miss Thee 83

Introduction

I hate to admit it, but I sometimes make excuses when I don't want to do something. Many times that has cost me more than I care to share.

Life can be so crazy at times that I don't know what I should do. My plan is to enjoy life as presented to me each day. I only have one shot at each day and then I must move on to the next.

I want to get the most out of each day and I know laughter is the best way to do that.

Sure, I have made mistakes, but I have learned more from my mistakes than anything else.

This book is an illustration of how I handled my mistakes during the past year. I plan to do better next year.

Where Is The Gracious Mistress Of The Parsonage?

Our family's Christmas this year was the best one yet. But, of course, The Gracious Mistress of the Parsonage says that every year. I completely agree with her this year.

Our great-granddaughter served as the focal point of our Christmas this year. She assumed that position because she was born two weeks before Christmas. What a gift.

This is our second great-grandchild. The first one is in Ohio, and we don't get to see him very often. But this new great-granddaughter is only seven minutes from our house. I was to realize what a difference that would be.

My granddaughter's mother and grandmother are now there to support this precious little great-granddaughter.

The time our granddaughter's mother can spend with her granddaughter is limited because of her work schedule.

The great-grandmother, the Gracious Mistress of the Parsonage, is free to visit the great-granddaughter whenever she pleases. Her "free" does have a cost, and I would soon find out that cost.

Every time we visit, I have to pull the great-grandmother away. I'm not entirely sure how this great-granddaughter will affect her when she's a few months old and then a few years old because she's only a few weeks old now. So I need to get ready for that.

The previous week was an interesting one.

The Gracious Mistress of the Parsonage came to my office on Monday morning as I was working and said, "I'm going to visit my great-granddaughter, and I prepared lunch in the refrigerator for you in case I don't get back in time."

She sped off and drove to the great-granddaughter's house without waiting for any response from me.

It was a relatively quiet morning. I stopped to check the time and realized it was time to eat. When I entered the kitchen, it was completely dark and quiet. I then recalled her mentioning going to the great-granddaughter's house.

My lunch was in the refrigerator, just as she had predicted. So I took the lunch plate out of the fridge and sat in my chair to eat my meal. I then returned to the kitchen with my empty plate and entered my office to continue working on my day's project.

Because I had not heard any sounds coming from the other rooms of the house. I decided to check on the infamous great-grandmother. She wasn't anywhere in sight.

I hoped she didn't have an accident because I didn't know where she could be. That started to worry me. She's never been known to leave the house for an extended period without sending me a text or making a phone call. Did she have a problem of some sort?

I was ready to text her on my cell phone when I heard her pull into the driveway. Then, as she entered the door, she said, "I forgot what time it was. I was having so much fun...." Then she began story after story of time with her great-granddaughter that day.

When I woke up the following morning, her side of the bed was vacant. I assumed she awoke early to prepare breakfast. There was no one in the kitchen when I went there.

Looking around, I noticed a note on the refrigerator, "My great-granddaughter needed me this morning, so I dropped everything to go and help her. Make your own breakfast."

Making a meal was simple because I'm not much of a breakfast hound dog. So the coffee was the main component of my breakfast, and there was plenty of it.

When I stopped midway through the morning while working in my office, I heard no noise coming from the other parts of the house. Unless there was an emergency involving the great-granddaughter, I assumed my wife should have returned home by this point.

I started to worry about the welfare of that tiny infant. Why would The Gracious Mistress of the Parsonage be so preoccupied with her if nothing was wrong?

When lunchtime arrived, I made my lunch. There's nothing better than a peanut butter and jelly sandwich for lunch and a hot cup of coffee. So I returned to my desk after lunch to pick up on my work.

I paused and listened for a while after lunch, but there was only silence. I was starting to worry a little bit. Was the great-granddaughter ill, or did the great-grandmother get into some accident returning home?

Where is The Gracious Mistress of the Parsonage?

Then I heard her drive into the driveway, exit the car, and enter the house. Then, I asked, "Is the great-granddaughter having any problems?"

"Oh, the great-granddaughter is doing great," she said, beaming one of those smiles in my direction. "I spent the entire day with her and had a great time."

She then began a series of stories about herself and her great-granddaughter, giggling while she told me various details about that young baby.

After a few weeks, whenever I ask myself, "Where is The Gracious Mistress of the Parsonage?" I only have to think about that great-granddaughter. That's where she is.

I believe Solomon in the Old Testament had it right when he said, "Children's children are the crown of old men; and the glory of children are their fathers." (Proverbs 17:6).

Children are truly a blessing from God. But grandchildren and great-grandchildren are beyond blessing. It is God's reward He gives to those faithful parents.

I Screamed For Ice Cream And Got In Trouble

Trouble is not my middle name, although it sure could be; just ask The Gracious Mistress of the Parsonage.

I try to keep out of trouble, but my definition differs from my wife's. What she considers to be trouble is just about everything I do. I will not ask her how I can keep from doing what I do. I don't need that trouble.

If I could remember some of the trouble I've been in it probably could help me keep out of some new trouble. But of course, my "new trouble" is something I've done before, many times, according to someone in our house.

My thought is, and I am unanimous in this, without trouble, there is no real life. If you don't get into some trouble, then something is wrong.

Sometimes, according to my experience, trouble is worth it.

Well, sometimes it's worth it.

One of my routines at night is to have a nice cold bowl of ice cream. I don't care what flavor it is because I've never had any ice cream that I didn't like. The one I like best is the one I'm eating at the time.

The Gracious Mistress of the Parsonage is very good at buying my ice cream and is always looking for coupons or BOGO, for which she is rather famous.

Not long ago, she came into the house excited and laughing, as I'd never seen her laugh before. It took a while for her to calm down, but when she did, I was able to find out what she was all excited about.

At the one store where she usually gets groceries, she found, much to her surprise, ice cream that was buy one and get two free. Of course, that sure made her day, but it also made my day as well.

I wonder if that was a mistake, but if it was, she took advantage of that ice cream sale.

She's very cautious with how much ice cream I should eat. When she came home with this bargain, I tried to explain that this meant I could have twice the amount of ice cream as before.

When I said that, the smile on her face quickly evaporated, and looking at me, she said, "It does not mean anything of the sort. You will eat what ice cream I give you, and that's all."

Well, you can't fault me for trying. If you don't try, how do you know something isn't going to work?

I was happy that we had a nice supply of ice cream just in case of any emergency. One emergency that I was thinking of was an overwhelming hunger for ice cream. According to The Gracious Mistress of the Parsonage, this is not an emergency.

I am banking on the fact that because we have so many boxes of ice cream, I could sneak a bowl while she wasn't home, and she wouldn't know about it. After all, with all those boxes, how in the world can you keep count?

One day while she was away for the day, I broke into the freezer and got a nice cold bowl of ice cream. It was one of the most delicious bowls of ice cream I've had in a long time.

Of course, I washed the dish and put it back into the cupboard to avoid leaving any evidence.

I was in my office doing a little bit of work when she came home, and within 10 minutes, I heard her yelling, "Did you sneak any ice cream from the freezer today?"

How she found out, I do not know. After all these years of marriage, I'm beginning to think she has a little ghost in the house keeping track of my movements. I can't prove it, but I'm starting to feel it.

Every night around 8 o'clock, she gets ice cream for the both of us. Mine in a bowl and hers in a cone. I wouldn't have it any other way.

One night after supper, I sat in the living room watching a little TV. I noticed the clock said 8 o'clock, the time for the ice cream. So I waited a few minutes, and still, no ice cream showed up.

She was busy in her craft room with some crafts, and I just thought she had forgotten what time it was. That always happens to me, but it rarely happens to her. She knows what time it is a half-hour before the time. Figure that out.

Thinking I could solve the problem, which was a ridiculous ploy on my part, I decided to tell her what time it was.

With my strongest outdoor voice, I yelled, "It's ice cream time. Yes, I'll have ice cream."

She came to the living room, looked at me, and said, "Did you hear that terrible noise just a few moments ago?"

Shaking her head she then turned around and walked back to her craft room, and to my disappointment, there was no ice cream that night. So I was tempted to go to the freezer and get my ice cream, but I wasn't sure what kind of trouble I was in that night.

David seemed to understand this when he wrote, "God is our refuge and strength, a very present help in trouble" (Psalm 46:1).

No matter what my trouble is, because God is my refuge I have nothing to worry about.

What Would My Life Be Without A Cookie

This past week was about as crazy as they get. When I think it can't get any crazier, somebody hears me and makes it crazier just for me.

One morning I had to go across town to get some office supplies and other things. I try to ensure that when I go, it's for several things, not just one.

The traffic was somewhat crazy. Everybody was driving as though trying to escape some danger behind them. I don't like it when the traffic gets like this. I'm not sure why people drive the way they drive.

I must say, one of the craziest drivers seemed to be somewhat religious. He stuck his hand out the window and pointed toward heaven. Unfortunately, he got the wrong finger. It's the thought that counts.

Hearing a roaring noise behind me; I looked in my rearview mirror and saw a little red convertible zooming up past me, and behind the steering wheel was an older man looking like my grandfather. He had the biggest smile as he was roared past me. I guess he was living out his teenage years before he died, which could be soon.

Then there was a motorcycle zinging in and out and crossing the double line several times, and he whizzed by me, laughing like he was having the time of his life.

Carefully driving home to avoid getting hit, I began to think about this. Where do these people get their driver's licenses? Perhaps it's an online service, and they don't have to take any driving test. So I would like to get a hold of the person that gave them a driver's license, and shake my finger in his face.

Then I asked myself, who in the world sold a vehicle to these people?

Before I got home, I passed an accident along the way. I guess people don't know that there's a consequence in driving like an idiot. So again, where do idiots get driver's licenses?

The fact that I got home without any accident was a real blessing.

I was frustrated with all the nonsense on the highways. I come from Pennsylvania, and the most traffic is horse and buggy. So what would it be like if all vehicles, both gas and electric, were banned in our country and everybody had to drive a horse and buggy?

It ain't ever going to happen, but it was at least worth thinking about, as nervous as I felt at the time.

I finally arrived home, parked my vehicle, and went inside. The Gracious Mistress of the Parsonage met me as I walked in and said, "What happened? You look terrible."

Well, I did look in the mirror that morning, so I did look terrible, but that wasn't what she meant.

I told her about all the crazy drivers I had to deal with driving across town.

"Who," I said to her most frantically, "gave these people a driver's license?"

She looked at me sympathetically and smiled.

Then I said, "Who in the world sold them a vehicle thinking they could drive?"

She knew I was frustrated and tense with all of this nonsense on the road.

It wasn't anything new, but sometimes things have a way of building up.

I went into the living room, sat in my easy chair, and decided to watch a little TV to calm my nerves. I'm not sure what I was watching; I just wanted to take some time and unwind from the crazy day I had.

Then, The Gracious Mistress of the Parsonage brought me a nice hot cup of coffee.

"Here," she said. "Maybe this will calm you down a little."

I smiled and thanked her because nothing calms me down like a nice hot cup of coffee. Whoever invented coffee should get a Nobel Peace Prize.

I took one sip, and I could feel my nerves starting to unravel. How I love a cup of coffee!

Then, The Gracious Mistress of the Parsonage did something unexpected. She came in and brought me some cookies.

"Here, these cookies may help you calm down a little more."

She handed me not one but two cookies. This was something that had never happened in my life before.

I sat in my chair, sipped some more coffee, and then gently smelled those cookies. That morning my wife was making cookies for somebody, so the kitchen was full of the cookie aroma. Walking in, I was so stressed that I did not smell those cookies.

The aroma of that cookie seemed to fill me with good vibes, like it was 1969.

I took one bite and began slowly and delicately munching on that cookie. Nothing so wonderful in all the world as a freshly baked cookie. So I leaned back, closed my eyes, and enjoyed that cookie.

In no time, the first cookie was gone. Then I picked up the second cookie, looked at it with admiration, and began nibbling it.

As I was chewing that cookie, I thought to myself, what would life be without cookies?

In a rather relaxed mode, I remembered what the apostle Paul said. "The Lord give mercy unto the house of Onesiphorus; for he oft refreshed me, and was not ashamed of my chain" (2 Timothy 1:16).

It's amazing how God sends people into our lives to refresh us when we seem to be under some kind of stress.

Sow A Thought Reap A Pie

One thing that has been burning in my life has been thoughts. Not that I don't have thoughts, but I'm not quite sure how to use them when I have them. Looking back over my life, it has been my thoughts that got me into trouble. I just never learn.

I was finishing up a little project in my office, and I couldn't help but think about The Gracious Mistress of the Parsonage's wonderful coconut cream pie. She makes a lot of pies, but this one has to be her best. It's been a long time since she baked a coconut cream pie.

Being a husband as long as I have been, over 50 years, I know it doesn't do any good for me to tell my wife what to do, particularly in the kitchen. My access to the kitchen has to be supervised by her.

How can I get her to bake her infamous and delicious coconut cream pie?

This thought took a whole bunch of other thoughts to come up with a good idea. I don't always come up with a good idea, but I thought I had done it this time. I needed to plant a thought in her mind concerning this coconut cream pie.

How I was going to do this demanded some more thought, then I came up with an idea.

We get spam callers about medicare benefits and my expiring auto warranty, so I come up with a little idea. The next time someone like this calls me, I will use it to plant a thought into my wife's head.

It didn't take long, and one of those spam calls came.

Somewhere in the conversation, they asked me a question, and I noticed The Gracious Mistress of the Parsonage was in the next room within hearing distance.

I inserted into the conversation, "And my wife bakes the most delicious coconut cream pie I have ever eaten." I mentioned it several times in the conversation, hoping I had planted some thought in someone's mind.

The expiring car warranty call came, and I used that as an opportunity to say, "You should taste the amazing coconut cream pie that my wife bakes. You would love it."

I even used it when some friends called me. I would say, "Do you remember my wife's delicious coconut cream pie?"

This routine went on for a couple of weeks, and I hadn't noticed any difference with The Gracious Mistress of the Parsonage. I was beginning to feel that maybe my "sowing a thought" wasn't working. That thought in and of itself caused a little bit of despair on my side.

Giving this quite a bit of thought, I just couldn't come up with another scheme to entice her to bake coconut cream pie without knowing it was me.

I kept it up for several weeks, hoping that one little thought might take root. It was worth the trouble if I got one of her coconut cream pies at the end.

One day this past week, I had several appointments across town that would take up most of the day. So, I would be out of the house all that time, unable to sow any more thoughts.

It was a long and boring day, but finally, it was over, and I headed home. I pulled into the driveway, got out, and entered the house. As I entered, there was this familiar aroma that I really couldn't place at the time. It smelled delicious, but I didn't quite understand what it was.

My wife was in the kitchen, so I went into my office and sat at my desk to finish my day's task.

It wasn't long before The Gracious Mistress of the Parsonage came to the doorway into my office with something in her hand. Then she said, "Look what I baked this morning. It's a coconut cream pie. For some reason, I kept thinking about my coconut cream pie I made a couple of years ago. I don't know why, but I just decided to bake this pie this morning." Then she smiled at me.

I smiled back at her and said, "When can I have a piece of that delicious pie?"

She brought me a piece, and I sat there enjoying every bite. I was beginning to think that my planting the thought would not work.

After finishing that pie, I began thinking, is this pie the result of me planting a thought, or did she just hear what I was saying and was trying to trick me?

I never will know which way it was. But then I got to thinking; maybe I will try this again to get my wife to do something in the future. I'm going to have to give this an awful lot of thought because it's very hard to fool The Gracious Mistress of the Parsonage.

Sometimes my thoughts get me into trouble and sometimes they don't. I can never tell which way any of thoughts will go.

I thought about what David said, "Search me, O God, and know my heart: try me, and know my thoughts: And see if there be any wicked way in me, and lead me in the way everlasting" (Psalm 139:22-24).

It is important for me to allow God to search me and know my thoughts and if there is any thing that offends God, I need to deal with regularly.

Ugly Isn't For Sissies

Over the years of marital bliss, we've not had many disagreements. She likes broccoli. I like Apple Fritters. We've never been able to come to any agreement with that. But, outside of that, everything has been rather smooth.

There's one controversy that has plagued our house for the last few years, and there doesn't seem to be any solution. There are some problems with no solutions, and I guess this is one of them.

The controversy I have is about my bathroom mirror; each of us has our bathroom with our own mirror. My mirror has some very significant issues with it.

For several years I have suggested that we replace my old mirror with a new one.

Once, I even suggested I would be glad to pay for the new mirror out of my Apple Fritter account, which was a mistake.

When I said that, she looked at me with a long pause and then said, "You have an account for Apple Fritters?"

I knew I was in trouble for that; I guess I kissed my Apple Fritter account goodbye.

The controversy I had is that my old mirror portrays me as some old guy. I find it rather frustrating because I have some pictures of myself, and I don't look old at all.

As we discussed this, she said, "My mirror portrays me as I really am." She smiled one of her sarcastic smiles at me.

"Let me," I said, "go and look in your mirror to see if what you're telling me is really true."

I entered her bathroom and was surprised as I looked in her mirror and saw some old guy looking back at me.

Immediately I went out and said, "Hey, who's that old guy in your bathroom?"

She laughed and said, "I think it's you, but all I ever see is some old lady."

"I am not that old," I demanded.

I then went and got our family photo album, brought it back, opened it up, pointed to a picture, and said, "See, that's me."

She looked at the picture, then back at me laughingly, and said, "Yes, that's you when you were in high school."

I flipped a few pages and said, "There I am."

"That's our wedding picture," she said with a smile.

By that time, I was just a little bit frustrated. If I look at those pictures and then look in the mirror, I do not see any resemblance whatsoever. How can that old rascal in the mirror be me?

The Gracious Mistress of the Parsonage could see that I was just a little bit discouraged. After all, pictures don't lie, but I think mirrors do.

"Don't you realize that as we grow and get older, our looks change?"

Looking at her, I was shaking my head and unwilling to reach her level of understanding.

"But," I complained, "I'm not that old looking, am I?"

Then she handed me a more recent photograph. It was me holding my granddaughter on the day of her birth. I looked at it as though I was looking out for the first time. When I first looked at it, I didn't see myself; rather, I saw my great-granddaughter.

After looking at it for a few moments, I sat back in my chair and sighed deeply. "So, I am an old man."

"Well, my dear, you're not young anymore."

I stared at her for a few moments and then said, "Tell me, why do you look so good, and I look so old?"

"Because you're not looking in my bathroom mirror."

"Maybe," I said, "we could change bathroom mirrors?"

She started laughing and a few moments later, I joined her in laughing.

This was the first time I ever seriously looked at myself.

In the morning, when I go to the bathroom to comb my hair, shave, and brush my teeth, I ignore what's in the mirror. Maybe I ought to.

Thinking about this for a bit, I had a thought. Does it really matter how old a person looks? After all the only cure for not getting old is dying.

I've noted lately that some of these Hollywood stars get facelifts, tummy tucks, and all sorts of changes to their body. I wonder if they do that for themselves or for the public that's looking?

Does it really matter how a person looks?

I believe the next time I'm in my bathroom, I'm going to have a little chat with that old guy in the mirror. I will say, "I don't care how old you look. You don't scare me." I had to rehearse that line a dozen times to get it right. I'm not sure I can trust that old guy in the mirror.

Of course, one of the great benefits is that I don't have to see how I look throughout the day. The people on the other side of my glasses have that to handle.

I have learned to appreciate what God said to Samuel in, 1 Samuel 16:7, "But the Lord said unto Samuel, Look not on his countenance, or on the height of his stature; because I have refused him: for the Lord seeth not as man seeth; for man looketh on the outward appearance, but the Lord looketh on the heart."

God does not judge me by my outward appearance, but by my heart. If my heart isn't right with God nothing else really matters.

Another Celebration In The Bank

This month The Gracious Mistress of the Parsonage and I celebrate the 52nd anniversary of our engagement. In August, it'll be the 52nd anniversary of our wedding.

I can't believe we have been together for 52 years. But, alas, here it is.

I first met her in September of 1970 when I went to Bible college. Knowing that God was calling me to be a pastor, I understood that I would need a wife to help me in this ministry.

Not being woman-wise, and no dating experience: I thought a date was simply a dried-up prune.

Not knowing what to do, I simply put it in God's hands. Before I went to this Bible college, my prayer was, "Heavenly Father, make the first young lady I meet when I go to school be the wife you have chosen for me."

It sounds ridiculous, but not being woman-wise, it was my best choice.

My parents took me up to New York, where the college was, as we drove into the men's dorm driveway a young lady was coming out. This young lady had her hair rolled up in tomato cans which was rather usual at that time.

When I saw her walk out, I quickly prayed, "Not yet, Father. My feet have not touched the ground."

I think God was chuckling. For some reason, I was never able to get away from her because it was a very small college, and everybody knew everybody.

Not being woman-wise, I did not know how to conduct myself in such a situation.

In December, we were on some date, and she happened to say, or so I thought she happened to say it, "Wouldn't it be nice to get married?"

Again, my not being woman-wise did not allow me to understand what was going on. I simply replied to her, "I think it would be great to get married."

Foolish me, I thought that was the end of the conversation.

The next day in school, as I walked down the hallway, everybody looked at me, smiled, and said, "Congratulations." So I smiled back and thanked them.

I had no idea what I was being congratulated on, I thought perhaps I finally passed a test in school.

After a while, I stopped somebody congratulating me and asked what he was congratulating me for.

Laughing, he said, "Oh, you silly boy. I'm congratulating you on your upcoming wedding." Then he walked away.

I stood in the hallway for a moment, trying to process what he had just told me.

What wedding was he talking about? Who did they think I was marrying?

Later that afternoon, I met her in the cafeteria, she looked at me, smiled, and said, "I've told everybody, and everybody is happy for us. Isn't it wonderful?"

I then realized I was the last one in the college that knew I was getting married.

God was the first one to know whom I was going to marry, and I was the last one to know. That is chapter 1 in woman-wise psychology.

Although it's been 52 years, I still have not progressed to chapter 2.

Perhaps chapter 2 would begin with, "Do you want to be right or happy?"

I am here to tell you that during those 52 years, I have been happy.

According to tradition back then, the next step was to get permission from her father to marry his daughter. So you understand I was rather nervous along this line because I had never met her father or mother.

Before the engagement, we traveled back to visit her family. It was then that I met her father.

I took him aside and said, "Sir, I would like to ask your permission for your daughter's hand in marriage."

He looked at me with a rather strange look and said, "No."

At this point, my flabber just got gasted, and I didn't know what to say.

He looked at me strangely and said, "Young man, you take my entire daughter or none of her. Not just her hand."

At this point, I realized I was also not father-in-law-wise. That was well beyond my pay scale. My heart sank, and I did not know the next step.

Looking at me, her father finally broke down laughing. I had no idea what he was laughing about.

"Of course, you can have my daughter's hand in marriage as long as you take the rest of her."

I tried to laugh as best I could but had no idea what was happening in the world. If this is what I was marrying into, it will be a long voyage.

As we were driving back to school, the future Gracious Mistress of the Parsonage looked at me and said, "Well, what do you think of my family?"

I just smiled back at her and she said, "Welcome to my family."

I smiled and thought about my favorite life verse from the Bible.

Proverbs 3:5-6, "Trust in the Lord with all thine heart; and lean not unto thine own understanding. In all thy ways acknowledge him, and he shall direct thy paths."

This verse has guided me throughout my entire life, especially in the area of marriage. Either I can lean on my own understanding, or, I can trust in the Lord with all my heart. If I'm going to go down the right path only God can lead me.

If I'm Not Crazy Nobody Is

Last Sunday, we were driving to our Sunday morning church service and encountered a lot of crazy drivers. As The Gracious Mistress of the Parsonage was driving, I kept my cool and, more importantly, my mouth closed.

Every once in a while, she would say, "What's wrong with these crazy drivers?"

I could tell she was a little agitated by these drivers swaying in and out of the lanes.

"Why are people so crazy when they are driving? How did they get a driver's license?"

Certainly, I could have enhanced the conversation, but I knew I would not come out on the winning side. There are times when a person should just keep their mouth shut. After all these years as a husband, I am learning more about keeping my mouth shut.

The Gracious Mistress of the Parsonage has often looked at me and said, "Are you crazy or what?"

You don't know how often I wanted her to define what she meant by "or what." But, of course, I'm not sure I would have liked her definition at that time.

I'm unsure if I was born crazy or just learned it as I grew up. But the facts remain that I am crazy in a variety of ways.

It would be nice to sit down with The Gracious Mistress of the Parsonage and get her to explain how she thinks I am crazy. I'm not sure she could ever stop talking about it if I did.

Some people's crazy is another person's lifestyle. So I'm leaning towards the latter.

Not long ago, she had to go thrift store shopping which would take up most of her day. I was rather excited because I've been thinking about getting an Apple Fritter for several weeks. These are not on my diet, and I'm not allowed to bring them into the house.

A few minutes after she left, I jumped in my truck, went, got an Apple Fritter and brought it home. I was in Apple Fritter heaven.

On my third bite of that Apple Fritter, I heard the front door open, and in walked The Gracious Mistress of the Parsonage. She stopped, looked at me with both hands on her hips, and said, "Are you crazy or what? You're not allowed to have Apple Fritters, especially in this house."

Well, when you're crazy, I guess you're crazy.

I've been thinking about this, and the thought that has dominated my thinking is, what's so wrong about being crazy? Some of the best people I know are crazy.

Driving home from church about three weeks ago, some old man on a motorcycle was weaving back and forth, passing cars. When he passed us, he was smiling like a really crazy man.

When my wife saw him, she looked at me and said, "What is wrong with that crazy man?"

I laughed and wanted to say, but I didn't, "Well, that crazy man is just having fun. He's enjoying his life."

Looking at me, she might have said, "He better enjoy it now because that crazy guy isn't going to last very long."

I would have loved to stop him and query him, "Sir, what does your wife think of your driving like a crazy man?" I would have loved his answer about that. I probably could have learned a lesson or two about being crazy myself.

The wise man was pretty close to accurate when he said, "Crazy is as crazy does."

I remember once getting in trouble with The Gracious Mistress of the Parsonage.

I was in my easy chair reading a book, she came in very anxious and said, "Have you seen my glasses? I can't find them."

I looked at her and assumed this was a trick question and she was setting me up for something because her glasses were on the top of her head. I didn't know where this "joke" was going, but I thought I would just play along.

Looking at her, I said, "Are you crazy or what?" Then I laughed hysterically as she stared at me.

"I am not crazy; I just cannot find my glasses." She wasn't laughing.

Looking through the living room, she finally reached to the top of her head and said, "Oh, here they are on top of my head. Why didn't you tell me? Are you crazy or what?"

It's crazy people like me that have all the fun in the world from people who don't think they're crazy. There's not a day in the week that I would ever suggest to The Gracious Mistress of the Parsonage that I thought she was crazy. I do think that way, but I will never expose that thought to her because I love my life as it is.

What would life be without a little bit of craziness?

From my long experience with being crazy, I have concluded that being crazy is an art. It takes a long time to learn how to be crazy, and I think I am very close to a Ph.D. in crazyolgy.

I couldn't help but think of my favorite Bible verse. Proverbs 3:5-6, "Trust in the Lord with all thine heart; and lean not unto thine own understanding. In all thy ways acknowledge him, and he shall direct thy paths."

No matter how crazy the world around me is, I can trust God to lead me in the right direction.

Who's Been Fiddling With My Mind?

When it comes to music, I am an amateur in many regards. I signed up for a violin class in first grade and took lessons. After about a month, the teacher met with my parents and begged them to pull me from that class.

He said, "Out of deep respect for music, this boy should not play the violin."

I can't think of anybody in my immediate family that plays any instrument or has any skill in music. I thought I would be the first one, but I wasn't.

The Gracious Mistress of the Parsonage is a different story. Many people on her side of the family are involved in music, and her father was a great piano player and could play the piano with no music set before him.

Also, his daughter plays the piano, organ, flute, and harp. As long as I've been a pastor, she has played the piano in all our church services. She is very gifted along that line, and I'm so happy.

I confess that I am not musically inclined, and I am unanimous in that opinion.

It's not that I don't like music; I cannot replicate it with these vocal cords that God gave me. So I guess His plan was for me not to sing.

Music is very relaxing for me, and even though I cannot sing, I can listen to music with great appreciation.

The one thing that bugs me is early in the morning, whether it's television or radio, I hear a song and can't get it out of my head. All day, that music buzzes in my head, and I can't get it to stop.

We took a trip not long ago, and The Gracious Mistress of the Parsonage drove her Sissy Van, while I sat in the passenger side. For some reason a song got in my head, I can't remember which one, but I heard it over and over again.

I heard it so many times that I began to sing that song under my breath, which was not a very good thing to do.

I have a way of humming and singing a song simultaneously, coming out naturally.

As I got to singing, suddenly, The Gracious Mistress of the Parsonage pulled over, stopped her van, looked at me, and said, "Are you having some kind of spasm?" She looked very serious as she said it.

I looked at her seriously, having no idea what she was talking about.

"You're not sick, are you?"

I began to understand her alarm, and I cautiously said, "I'm okay; I was just singing."

"Oh my," she said, "it sounded like you were on your last road trip to death."

I don't know where that came from.

She then encouraged me not to hum or sing along the way.

I didn't realize I was singing out loud. I thought it was just in my head. But being the kind of husband I am, I kept my mouth shut for the rest of the trip.

The only place I sing is in the shower because there's nobody there, and nobody can hear me, and I can do my thing.

The other day as I was showering, I did not realize The Gracious Mistress of the Parsonage was within hearing distance. I try to take a shower when she's not home and cannot hear me. There's a reason for that.

As so I got into my shower a song began to rumble in my head, and within a few seconds, I started singing. Boy, was I singing and enjoying every note.

Suddenly, I heard a rapid knock on the bathroom door and my wife saying, "Are you okay? You didn't fall in the shower, did you? Do you need any help?"

At first, I couldn't figure out what was happening when it dawned on me that I was singing and she was hearing.

Oh "No, my dear," I said quite loudly, "I was just singing."

I heard a profound sigh on the other side of the bathroom door, and heard her say, "Don't scare me like that again."

I do try to control my singing and keep it from crossing my lips.

Music does have a way of controlling me. Some music makes me sad, and some makes me glad. The problem is music that's in my head controls me in some way.

I go into a store, and they're playing music, and come out of that store with the music playing in my head, and I'm humming along the way. Driving home in my truck alone, I sing as loudly as possible, knowing nobody can hear me. But, of course, sometimes I forget to stop and walk into the house singing, and you can only guess the kind of trouble it presents to me.

If only I could remember to keep my thoughts especially those musical thoughts in my head and far away from my tongue I would have a happier life.

Thinking about this all little I was reminded of what King Solomon said in Proverbs 29:11, "A fool uttereth all his mind: but a wise man keepeth it in till afterwards."

That wise old man knew what he was talking about. I know there's a time to speak but there's also a time to keep quiet. For me it's a challenge to differentiate between the two. The quieter I am the less difficulties I encounter

Nothing Like A Mystery To Calm My Nerves

Nothing calms me down more than a mystery when I have a busy week.

The other afternoon I got caught up and faced some rather stressful situations. The remedy to all of this would be to watch one of those mystery movies.

One was playing that afternoon, so I decided to rearrange my schedule, enjoy the afternoon watching that mystery movie with a nice hot cup of coffee, and maybe adding an Apple Fritter to it makes it even more restful.

As I began watching this mystery, the first part is always the murder. So who was it that committed this murder? That is the detective's job to find out the murderer.

As these mystery movies begin, I like to guess who the real murderer is. I am usually wrong but don't tell anybody, especially The Gracious Mistress of the Parsonage.

Getting involved in the story, the detectives brought in one suspect they believed committed the crime.

I was getting involved when I heard someone walk into the living room; it was The Gracious Mistress of the Parsonage. She looked at the TV, then back at me and said very firmly, "He is not the murderer. The wife is the one who murdered her husband."

Then she turned around and returned to do her kitchen work.

I chuckled a little because how would she know who the murderer was at this point in the movie?

Watching this, the detectives finally concluded that the subject they were interviewing was not the one who did the murder.

Then they came up with another suspect, and as they were interviewing him, a head popped into the living room; it was The Gracious Mistress of the Parsonage. "He's not the guilty one; the wife killed her husband; trust me on this."

Of course, if anybody knows what wives are capable of, it would be her.

I knew she was wrong about the wife killing her husband. They had interviewed this wife, who had a good alibi; the detectives crossed her off the suspect list.

They brought in several more suspects, and they were all cleared as far as the crime. Finally, they got to the place where no other suspects were in view.

Suddenly, someone appeared as a suspect that they did not see before.

That's the way a good mystery goes. The one they had seemed like a very good prospect. He had no credible alibi at the time of the murder.

The more they interviewed him, the more it seemed like he was the murderer.

Watching it, I began to agree that they finally got their murderer. All they had to do was collect the evidence needed to convict him.

Just then, a head popped into the living room. "He did not do the killing," she said very emphatically. "As I said before, the wife killed her husband."

I did not know how she came up with that because she was working in the kitchen, and I was watching the television. So how could she know things about the mystery I didn't know?

"You're wrong," I said to her, "all the evidence points to this one they just arrested. No other person has his evidence."

She poked her head back in, and I said, "The wife is not in the picture right now. She could not have done the crime."

With one of her smiles, she replied, "Trust me. The wife did it. If I'm right, I'll bet you lunch tomorrow at my favorite restaurant."

Could I pass up something like that? All the evidence pointed to that person, and none to the wife.

"I will take you up on that bet, and I can't wait to have lunch at my favorite restaurant tomorrow."

Walking back into the kitchen, I could hear her chuckling. I had never known her to be wrong like this, and I was preparing myself for a grand celebration at my favorite restaurant tomorrow for lunch. This will be the first time I have ever won a bet against her. I must jot this down and record it because it may never happen again.

Returning to the mystery movie, suddenly, everything began to change. The man they thought did the crime had an airtight alibi, then the unthinkable happened.

The alibi of the wife began to break down as the detectives re-examined the evidence; they saw it differently to their surprise.

As it turned out, all the evidence revealed the wife killed her husband, and she was the murderer.

I heard some chuckling from the kitchen area and wasn't going to ask what was happening. I knew exactly what was going on.

At lunch, the next day, all The Gracious Mistress of the Parsonage could do was smile as she read through the menu and placed her order with the waitress.

I've never known her to order so much for lunch.

Driving home from the restaurant, I happen to think of a verse of Scripture found in

Matthew 11:28-30. "Come unto me, all ye that labour and are heavy laden, and I will give you rest. Take my yoke upon you, and learn of me; for I am meek and lowly in heart: and ye shall find rest unto your souls. For my yoke is easy, and my burden is light."

If I want real rest from my labors, it will only come from my relationship with Jesus Christ. Nothing can compromise that rest.

Learning What "me-time" Is All About

Several months ago, The Gracious Mistress of the Parsonage said she and her daughter and granddaughter were going to St. Augustine for a week and wondered if I wanted to go along.

I said, "Let me think about it for a while, and I'll get back to you."

I then overheard a conversation between my wife and her daughter concerning their trip to St. Augustine. One phrase that kept coming up in that conversation was "thrift stores." That caught my attention.

If there's a place I do not like to be, it is a thrift store. However, the Gracious Mistress of the Parsonage is an expert in everything thrift store.

The week before she went, she asked me if I wanted to go along with them. She smiled and said, "After all, we will be spending a lot of time at the thrift stores in the area."

I was not too fond of her smile on this occasion; I knew exactly what it meant.

Thinking about how to get out of the situation, I told her, "No, I don't think I want to go; there are some things I need to do here, so you girls go and have a great time."

"What is it that you need to do?"

I said as seriously as possible, "I need to spend some Me-Time here by myself."

"Me-Time," she said as she laughed. "Do you need any advice on how to do that activity?"

The week of the "girl's trip" had arrived, and The Gracious Mistress of the Parsonage had her Sissy Van packed for the trip. I noticed a large empty spot in the back, but I didn't say anything to her about it. I knew exactly the purpose of that space.

Finally, she said goodbye, kissed me, and was out the door to begin the trip to St. Augustine.

Early the following day, I began doing some of my projects for the week. I had some books that needed reading, and started my work.

A little after noon, I checked my watch and wondered where lunch was. Usually, by this time, The Gracious Mistress of the Parsonage has lunch ready. So I got up and went into the kitchen to see what was holding her up.

When I got into the kitchen, it dawned on me that I was involved in "Me-Time" for the week. I'm not sure I had included lunchtime in my preparation for this week.

I opened the refrigerator, picked out some things for lunch, and enjoyed my lunch. The Gracious Mistress of the Parsonage had prepared many things in the fridge for this week, so I took advantage of her generous preparations.

As I was munching on my lunch, I was thinking about this "Me-Time" that I thought was wonderful. But at least I had lunch, and then I could return to what I was doing.

At suppertime, it was the same routine. As I ate my supper, I couldn't help but think that this "Me-Time" wasn't worth the time. But I was in the middle of it, so there was nothing I could do, but it did help me with an excuse not to go to St. Augustine.

I put in a lot of hard work and finally went to bed.

I must've slept very well that night because before I knew it, morning arrived, and time to get up and have breakfast. I noticed it was empty on the other side of the bed, and I just thought that she had gotten up ahead of me and was getting everything ready for breakfast.

I walked out to the kitchen, and there was nobody in the kitchen. So I wondered where she could have been and how soon she would have breakfast.

Looking out the front window, I noticed her Sissy Van was missing, and then it dawned on me.

She's not here, and I'm on my "Me-Time" misadventure. I'm on my own for today.

The first thing I had to do was to make the coffee. So how can you start a day without coffee?

Looking around, I could not see any coffee, only an empty coffee pot on the counter. Now, I had to figure out how to work that coffee pot.

I found the coffee grounds for the coffee pot. I didn't know how much to put in, so I put in a lot because I like a nice hot cup of coffee. Then I put water where it was supposed to go and thought I had everything well done.

With my fingers crossed, I pressed the start button and the coffee pot, and nothing happened. Now, what was I supposed to do? As I moaned over this, I noticed that the coffee was unplugged. The Gracious Mistress of the Parsonage seems to unplug the coffee pot every night before bed.

I sighed a deep sigh and plugged it in and pressed the button in the coffee pot started to work.

That was just the beginning of "Me-Time," and much more was happening.

After two days of this, I realized all the work that The Gracious Mistress of the Parsonage did that I was unaware of.

Giving this a lot of thought, I was reminded of the verse of Scripture. "Can two walk together, except they be agreed?" (Amos 3:3).

Maybe instead of focusing on "Me-Time" it would be much better to focus on "We-Time." There is much more advantageous to this.

I'm So Poor I Can't Pay Attention

Occasionally I go to my computer and search for the wealthiest preachers in America. I am curious to know who came up with this idea, but I check it out occasionally to see who they are.

As often as I have checked this information, I have never found my name on that list. I so much wanted to see my name on that list. Everybody knows that the Internet never lies. So, I need to accept that I am not one of the wealthiest preachers in America. Poor me!

That may explain many things in my life that I did not quite understand before.

When traveling in the Sissy Van, The Gracious Mistress of the Parsonage is always behind the steering wheel. I make it a point not to drive that Sissy Van anymore than I have to.

As we drive, my wife will say, "Did you see that car? They're from Idaho."

Of course, I did not see it because I was not paying attention. When The Gracious Mistress of the Parsonage drives, she focuses on everything within her focus. Even when driving my truck, and she is in the passenger seat, she sees everything around her.

Do not let this get back to her, but she sees things that I do not think exist. I will never contest her on that subject.

Unlike my wife, I don't have that much focus to see everything that is happening around me.

Once when she asked me if I saw something, I replied, "No, I'm just too poor to pay attention."

I laughed, of course, but she didn't think it was funny.

Driving across town to church one Sunday morning, she said, "Did you see that sign? What did it say?"

I didn't see it, so I responded, "I'm sorry, but I'm too poor to pay attention." Then I chuckled.

She just threw me one of her infamous grimaces.

For some reason, she believes I should pay attention to everything around me. I don't know why because I'm not interested in many of the things around me. And, I am too poor to pay attention.

While driving to an appointment the other day, I asked, "Could I borrow a dollar from you?"

She looked at me quizzically and said, "Why do you need a dollar from me?"

"Oh," I said softly, "I just need some money to pay attention while you're driving."

She did not respond to me; of course, she never gave me that dollar. So I tried to explain to her that it is very expensive to pay attention. I don't think she believed me.

Several weeks later, we went to our Sunday morning church service, and I noticed a license plate and said, "Look at that license plate. They're from Montana."

There was silence on the other side of the car, and finally, she looked at me and said, "Where did you get that dollar?"

I had no idea what she was talking about, so I just said, "What dollar are you talking about?"

She snickered like I had not heard her snicker in a long time and said, "You know, the dollar so that you can pay attention."

The only thing I can say is that she has enough money to pay attention to everything, even some things I don't know.

Having enough money to pay attention to everything around you must be nice. I'm sure my life would change if I could afford to pay attention to everything.

The Gracious Mistress of the Parsonage can pay attention even when fast asleep. One time we were taking a trip to St. Augustine. She leaned back in her side and took a nap. At least, I thought she was asleep.

I was coming to where I needed to turn, but I wasn't sure if this was the right place. As I slowed down, I heard The Gracious Mistress of the Parsonage say, "No, you need to turn at the next light."

Looking over, I saw her eyes were closed, and it looked like she was sound asleep. She is rich enough to pay attention even when she is sound asleep.

I often wonder where she has all this money, probably in the Central Bank of Mind Your Own Business.

Watching television, suddenly, The Gracious Mistress of the Parsonage said, "Did you see that? I wonder who that is?"

I begin to say, "No...." My wife jumped in and said, "I know, dear, you're too poor to have paid attention."

Boy, has she got me figured out? I'm going to have to open up some kind of a savings account, maybe a little piggy bank, and try to save up enough money to finance my poor attention. So far, The Gracious Mistress of the Parsonage has refused to loan me money for this cause.

During my Bible reading recently, I read 1 Timothy 6:9-10, "But they that will be rich fall into temptation and a snare, and into many foolish and hurtful lusts, which drown men in destruction and perdition. For the love of money is the root of all evil: which while some coveted after, they have erred from the faith, and pierced themselves through with many sorrows."

Being rich does have its challenge, which I will never face. The disturbing aspect of this passage is where Paul says, "the love of money is the root of all evil." That is my temptation.

What A Wacky World We Live In

I like the old saying, "Just when you think it can't get any worse, it does."

This is the kind of world we live in today, and I'm still not adjusted to this sort of thing. I'm not sure I will ever adjust to the world around me.

The Gracious Mistress of the Parsonage and I will be watching the news, and a story of some devastation somewhere in the world will come on.

When this happens, The Gracious Mistress of the Parsonage will say, "What a wacky world we live in." And if anybody knows about wacky, it is she. After all, she married me.

A story happened in our city when a truck driver was driving under an overpass, and the truck was too big and smashed the overpass. That shut down traffic for at least one day.

"What's wrong with that driver?" The Gracious Mistress of the Parsonage asked. "Doesn't he know about overpasses?"

Then she sighed deeply and said, "What a wacky world we live in."

When I was young, we had the Three Stooges. Today we have the news media, and I'm unsure which one is wackier.

Watching the news the other night, a similar story was being reported, and I looked at my wife and said, "What a wacky world we live in." I paused for a moment and then said, "It's not the world I grew up in." Then I laughed.

I wasn't expecting her response, but after all this time, I should've expected something.

"Whatever made you think that you have grown up?"

I didn't catch it at first, but I got what she said after a while.

That gave me pause for thinking, have I really grown up?

When I was a teenager at home, my mother would get aggravated at me and say very dramatically, "Why don't you just grow up?"

Now, after over 50 years, my wife is questioning that I have grown up.

After she said it to me, I pondered for quite a few days on what does it actually mean to grow up? And, most importantly of all, does anybody ever grow up?

We may live in a wacky world because few people have actually grown up yet. So if we had more adults around, maybe things wouldn't get as wacky as it has become.

I wanted to ask The Gracious Mistress of the Parsonage, who I assume has grown up, what I need to do to grow up?"

As we watched the news one night, she said, "What a wacky world we live in." At that point, I replied, "Maybe it's so wacky because people haven't grown up yet."

She went on a tirade explaining why most people have not grown up yet. I tried to listen carefully and take a few notes, but none made sense. It's like a first-grader listening to a 12th-grader explaining the law of gravity. That makes no sense to them at all.

I thought maybe I could get a few clues as to what I can do to grow up.

I couldn't keep it any longer, so I asked her, "What do you think I need to do to grow up?"

I should never ask questions like this to The Gracious Mistress of the Parsonage.

"Well," she started, "you should stop acting like a silly person."

I chuckled and said, "But what if I'm not acting?"

Staring at me, she said, "That is exactly what I mean."

"So, if you are not acting, you are the silliest person I have ever known."

According to her, you can't be silly and grown-up at the same time.

I asked her for more ideas about growing up.

"The next thing you need to do is stop thinking every situation is a joke."

Pondering this, I'm not sure I will ever grow up if that is true. I see a joke where The Gracious Mistress of the Parsonage sees something serious. She's much more grown-up than I ever will be.

"There is a positive side to this wacky world of ours." The Gracious Mistress of the Parsonage looked at me smiling. Then she continued, "If the world weren't as wacky as it is, people would see that you're wacky."

I did not know what she meant by that and would not press that point. The fact that she mentioned that is a plus for me, and I won't undermine that.

After all of this, I wonder if it's worth growing up. What good does it do to grow up when those people around you aren't? Maybe wacky is not that bad.

On the bright side, I'm going to try.

I couldn't help but think of one of the strangest stories about David in 1 Samuel 21, "And he [David] changed his behaviour before them, and feigned himself mad in their hands, and scrabbled on the doors of the gate, and let his spittle fall down upon his beard. Then said Achish unto his servants, Lo, ye see the man is mad: wherefore then have ye brought him to me? Have I need of mad men, that ye have brought this fellow to play the mad man in my presence? Shall this fellow come into my house?"

David used "wacky" to his advantage. That worked for him and after giving some thought, maybe that could work for my advantage. Of course, David was acting and I probably am not.

Has Anyone Seen My Marbles?

Whenever a week goes by without any hitches, I have learned that something somewhere is wrong.

I have lived long enough to realize that problems are a part of life. Most of my were created by me. I guess I'm a great creator in that regard. I don't think there is any reward for that kind of creativity.

The Gracious Mistress of the Parsonage is exceptionally educated in this area of my mistakes. She could receive the Nobel Peace Prize. She can recognize one of my mistakes two days before it even happens. I don't know how she does that and probably never will find out.

Whenever I screw something up, she always responds, "Have you lost your marbles?"

Initially, I didn't know I had marbles, nor did I understand what marbles were. But as I grew as a husband, I began to understand what she meant by marbles. I didn't know I had as many marbles as I had lost over the last 20 years.

One morning last week, I got up before The Gracious Mistress of the Parsonage and went out and got my coffee, I saw the kitties out on the porch looking in, so I opened the door, and they came marching in. What a great time they had together. As I was going to feed them, I heard a familiar voice down the hallway, "Have you lost your marbles? Get those cats out of here."

Of course, I didn't have to get the cats out because they ran for fear when they saw her coming down the hallway. I just stood there looking at the floor, trying to find my missing marbles.

Life has ups and downs, and I'm unsure which is better or worse. But throughout my life, I have never been helped in any situation by my marbles. How do my marbles help me in my everyday life? After all, my life has not changed much during these years of losing my marbles.

If I had more appreciation for my marbles, maybe, just maybe, I would not be getting in as much trouble with The Gracious Mistress of the Parsonage. Her obsession with marbles is beyond my ability to comprehend.

If I still have one or two marbles left maybe I could figure out how I can get back at her.

We had a doctor's appointment last week, so she drove her Sissy Van, and I sat over on the passenger side. It's hard for me to get in and out of that Sissy Van, but it saves me gas money for my truck.

As we were going down the street, I looked at her and said, "Have you lost your marbles? You missed the street we were supposed to turn on."

Inside I was laughing hilariously, but she did not share in that. She just looked at me and flashed one of her quirky smiles.

I sure do like it when a plan comes together.

One morning this week, I got up rather late and walked out to the living room in my pajamas. The Gracious Mistress of the Parsonage looked at me and said, "Have you lost your marbles? We have a breakfast appointment in about 10 minutes across town."

I had no idea, or at least I forgot about it, and maybe she was right; I did lose my marbles on this one.

I was thinking recently about how my life would change if I had all the marbles I lost. So what would my life be like at that point?

The other day as she was coming in the front door from a shopping trip I said to her, "Have you lost your marbles?"

Looking at me strangely, she said, "What are you talking about?"

Smiling back at her, I said, "Nothing, I just wanted to know if you had all your marbles together."

She didn't think that was funny and scowled at me and took the shopping bag into the kitchen.

If anybody has marbles, I think she does. So my question is simply, what is she doing with all those marbles?

I think I have one or two marbles left, and I was thinking of a plan for her birthday. I've been putting a lot of thought into it, and I'm almost done with the thinking aspect and about ready to put it all together.

I was in Wal-Mart the other day, and walking down one of the isles, I saw something that got my attention. There on the shelf were bags of marbles. It was the first time I ever saw marbles for sale. When I saw them, it gave me an idea. So I bought a bag of marbles.

This year I plan to give her a special birthday gift. It will be a box filled with marbles, wrapped in red paper with a lovely bow on the top.

When she opens it, I expect she will say, "Have you lost your marbles?"

I will respond, "No, my dear, I found your marbles."

I could not help but think of a Bible verse in Isaiah 55:8-9, "For my thoughts are not your thoughts, neither are your ways my ways, saith the Lord. For as the heavens are higher than the earth, so are my ways higher than your ways, and my thoughts than your thoughts."

God has never lost His "marbles." God shares His thoughts with us in the word of God.

The Princess Hath Thus Spoken

In December of last year, our second great-grandchild entered our family. Our first great-grandchild was a boy, and this one is a girl.

Like all our children, grandchildren and great-grandson, this great-granddaughter was a blessing to our family. If only children would stay young for the rest of their life! I have learned that the thing is to enjoy them while they are young.

Being retired, we have more time to spend with our grandchildren and great-grandchildren. I'm sure this is one of the great blessings that our Heavenly Father bestows upon us.

Because the mother of this great-grandchild, our granddaughter, is a working nurse, she went back to work following her maternity leave. That being the case, the grandma (mother) and great-grandma daycare operation kicked in.

These relationships get confusing, and I try to keep them separated. Still, the grandmother, our daughter, is also a working nurse and therefore does not have that much time for the daycare operation.

The great-grandmother, which is the Matriarch-Hierarchy, has more time for the daycare operation. That means the great-granddaughter is in our home quite often during the week.

I was pretty pleased with this arrangement and was glad to have a little great-granddaughter in our home as much as possible. Of course, you can never have too many of these little great-granddaughters.

After a few weeks I began to understand life as it is; I assumed things, but not always understanding, how they came into being.

At our family gathering, the new great-granddaughter was there and we were having our family dinner. Then something began to happen that at first, I did not quite understand, but later began to comprehend the whole issue in a different light.

The little great-granddaughter was sleeping in her bassinet in one of our bedrooms. We were chatting around the table, and then suddenly, we heard it.

Waa, Waa, Waa, Waa, Waa.

Being a man, I didn't quite understand what that noise was about. All of the ladies around the table got up and marched back to the bedroom with the little baby crying.

In a few moments, they all came out, and one was holding the baby while the rest were following. They all gathered in the living room, and I watched as they passed the baby around, and everybody had a chance to hold her.

It wasn't long before that little Princess stopped crying. And if I saw that right, if not smiling, at least she was snickering. At first, I did not quite understand what that was all about.

That was just the beginning.

Whenever The Gracious Mistress of the Parsonage babysat the great-grandbaby, I noticed a similar routine.

The great-grandmother got the great-grandbaby settled down, fed her, then quietly take her back, and put her in the bassinet in the bedroom. She fell asleep, and the great-grandmother tiptoed out of the bedroom and went to the kitchen to resume her work.

Then came that familiar sound from the bedroom.

Waa, Waa, Waa, Waa, Waa.

Before the second "Waa" got out, the great-grandmother turned her back on the kitchen and scooted back into the bedroom to bow before the great-granddaughter.

As she brought the little baby out, the baby looked at me and gave me one of her snickers. I am not sure, but I think she winked at me. Just do not let this get back to the great-grandmother.

So the great-grandmother cared for the baby, rocked it, and did everything babies need at that stage of life.

She finally went to sleep, and The Gracious Mistress of the Parsonage took the baby back to its bassinet to sleep for a little while.

When she came back, I was tempted, but I did not yield to that temptation, to ask her what all that crying was about. I was tempted, but I did not yield to that temptation, to tell her what I thought was going on.

It did not take long for the little Princess to do it all over again.

Waa, Waa, Waa, Waa, Waa.

Again, the great-grandmother dropped what she was doing and went back, got the baby out of the bassinet, brought her out, and fixed up a bottle for her lunch. So all the time, the little baby was smiling and giggling and then looking at me and winked; it seemed that way, at least from my perspective.

What I saw was the little Princess taking charge of her environment. How someone that young could know how to manipulate her environment is well beyond me. I should take a few notes from her.

Then I began thinking that perhaps this was the little Princess preparing to be a wife and mother, with the emphasis on the wife. If that is true, she has a great start at that.

I wonder what it is going to be like when this little Princess graduates to a teenager. Those are going to be the days, and I'm looking forward to them.

As I was pondering this situation I could not help but think of what that wise old man, Solomon, said in Proverbs 22:6, "Train up a child in the way he should go: and when he is old, he will not depart from it."

That wise old man understood that what a child becomes is a result of training. Too often the child dominates the training chair which predicts what happens when that child is old.

My Reward - I'll Eat It If I Want To

One day last week, I was up early working in my office as I normally do. I happened to pause what I was doing for a moment and smelled this wonderful aroma.

I know it wasn't me because I hadn't taken a shower yet. The aroma was coming from the kitchen area.

I got up from my desk, walked out into the kitchen and the closer I got the stronger that aroma was. It was so wonderful and I just could not get enough of it.

When I got to the kitchen there was The Gracious Mistress of the Parsonage baking cookies. Oh, how delicious those cookies smelled.

"What are you doing?" I asked.

"I'm baking cookies for some friends who are having a party tonight. They asked if I could bake them some cookies and I just couldn't refuse."

I smiled and just stared at all those cookies in the kitchen. There were molasses and peanut butter cookies, two of my favorites.

As I was looking at them, The Gracious Mistress of the Parsonage said to me rather sternly, "These cookies are not for you, they are for my friends. Do not eat them."

She saw me staring at those cookies and said, "Did you hear me?"

Then she told me that she had to go across town to pick up some things. So, she would be out of the house and I will be with the cookies all by myself. I can't think of a better scenario.

There's just no way I can be left alone with all those cookies in the kitchen and not eat some. I think my wife realized that and thought she could negotiate with me and solve the problem at hand.

Looking at me she said, "If you are a good boy today I will allow you to eat one cookie. Just one."

That brought me to quite a dilemma. What is her definition of "a good boy" and most importantly, how did she define "one cookie?"

I walked back to my office as she prepared to leave for the morning and I got back into the project I was working on. At least I tried to get back into my "saddle" for the morning, but it sure wasn't working for me.

No matter how hard I tried to concentrate on my project all I could think about was those delicious cookies out in the kitchen which I could smell in my office. I don't think it's fair that I should be put in such a situation.

After all, it's really not my fault. It is the fault of The Gracious Mistress of the Parsonage who makes cookies so delicious that I cannot refuse them. If it wasn't for that, I could ignore those cookies in the kitchen. So whatever happens, it is not my fault! And I am unanimous in that.

I then remembered that she said if I was a good boy I could have one cookie. That thought just ruminated through my mind and I couldn't handle it any longer and I had to go out into the kitchen and deal with it.

I think I'm a good boy, but that's only my evaluation. I sat for a moment at my desk and tried to think of anything bad I did that morning and I couldn't think of one thing. Therefore, with the evidence on the table, I have been a good boy today.

The next thing I had to deal with was the word "one." What does that word mean?

Looking at the cookies in the kitchen there were only two cookies: one was molasses and the other was peanut butter. So, in my understanding of the situation the word "one" means that I have to choose between the molasses cookie and the peanut butter cookie. That made sense to me.

So, according to my rationality, when I pick "one" cookie I can eat as many of them as I want to. I just can't eat the other one or I will be eating two cookies.

I can't tell you how happy I was in coming to this wonderful conclusion. I'm doing two things. I'm doing what my wife said to do and I am only eating one of the cookies. I love it when a plan comes together.

Going to the kitchen I made up my mind that the "one" cookie will be the peanut butter cookie. Oh, how I love her peanut butter cookies.

Picking out five cookies I joyfully skipped back to my office to enjoy these scrumptious treats. I earned these treats and therefore I'm going to eat them with a great deal of satisfaction.

I had finished those cookies and was working at my desk when I heard the front door open and expected it was The Gracious Mistress of the Parsonage.

I then heard her voice, "Did you eat all these cookies? When I told you to eat only one?"

Now I have some "splainin" to do.

A Bible verse came to mind that refreshed m concerning rewards. 2 John 1:8, "Look to yourselves, that we lose not those things which we have wrought, but that we receive a full reward."

There are times when I convince myself that I deserve a certain reward. All I need to do is twist certain words to my benefit thinking I deserve something when in fact I am not being honest.

I'd Rather Kiss
A Goat

There are very few things in my life I regret; at least that I can remember.

One of the good things about getting old is that you can forget many things. The important thing is to forget the right thing, which is a challenge. You can be sure I work on this all the time. It takes a really good memory to forget the right things.

What I regret the most is that The Gracious Mistress of the Parsonage never met my good old Uncle Fred. If she had met him, she would understand me more than she does today. She would understand why I am as crazy as I am. The problem is, she still would want to try to fix me.

One phrase I remember the most about Uncle Fred is, "I'd rather kiss a goat." I cannot tell you how many times I heard him say this. Where he got this phrase is a mystery to everyone who knew him.

If someone invited him to an activity he did not want to attend, he usually would respond by saying, "I'd rather kiss a goat."

People would smile because nobody had any idea what he was saying.

A friend once asked him, "Fred, will you watch the football game tonight?"

Looking at him as seriously as possible, Fred said, "I'd rather kiss a goat."

Knowing him as I did, he was not antisocial; he just liked to get under people's skin. Everything was a joke to him, and most people did not realize it. So they always took Uncle Fred seriously, which he wanted.

As a teenager, I spent time with him working in his garden one summer. He had a fantasy for garden work. If it could be planted, he would plant it. He had the best garden in the whole neighborhood at the time. Some plants in his garden I could not identify. Years later, much to my dismay, I found what some were, which explained a lot.

While spending time with him, I asked, "Uncle Fred, what do you mean when you say, I would rather kiss a goat? Do you really mean that?"

I had been thinking about this question for a long time, and at this point, I had the opportunity to ask him.

"Well, son," he said rather slowly, "it's a very interesting thing.

I have no idea what it means, and the people I say it to have no idea what I mean." He finished by laughing hysterically.

Then he explained that it was better to confuse people sometimes than try to explain something.

"For instance, if somebody wants you to do something and you don't want to do it but don't want to hurt their feelings, it's best to confuse them. That's where I come in and say, I'd rather kiss a goat."

According to him, he got out of many sticky situations by saying that.

"Just don't tell anybody I said that." He looked at me and then winked. I wondered if he was telling me the truth or just what he wanted me to know.

It was his way of getting along with people he liked but not doing what they wanted him to do.

It was the summer before Uncle Fred died that we had our family reunion. Just about everyone was there, and it was the last one that I got to go to.

Everyone was there except my grandfather. He was Fred's brother. Nobody knew where he was and was concerned because he never missed a family reunion.

Then, out of nowhere, my grandfather drove in, and in his truck was a goat. So he got out of the truck, brought the goat out, walked over to Fred, and said, "How about kissing this goat?"

Of course, Uncle Fred was stunned by the action, and everyone except Uncle Fred broke out in almost uncontrollable laughter.

Only my grandfather could pull one on Uncle Fred. I'm unsure how long it took him to put this kind of plan together, and he surely deserves credit.

I sure do miss Uncle Fred and wish The Gracious Mistress of the Parsonage would've had an opportunity to meet him. I'm afraid, though, she might've given him a goat to kiss but not what he had in mind.

Sometimes you don't really appreciate a person until after they're gone. The more I think of Uncle Fred, the more I appreciate his phrase, "I'd rather kiss a goat."

It all came to a head when the other day, The Gracious Mistress of the Parsonage came into my office and said, "Would you like to go shopping with the girls and me?"

Trying not to smile, I looked at her and said, "I'd rather kiss a goat."

Glaring at me with one of "those glares," she said, "What did you say? Did you just call me a goat?"

Oh boy, do I have some 'splainin' to do?

As I was trying to figure out my defense, I was reminded of what Jesus said in Matthew 12:36-37, "But I say unto you, That every idle word that men shall speak, they shall give account thereof in the day of judgment. For by thy words thou shalt be justified, and by thy words thou shalt be condemned."

The most important thing is to understand that God will hold me accountable for every word I speak, even those idle words.

Dizzy Is As Dizzy Says

Several years ago, I had a heart attack, which surprised my family and friends, who didn't know I had a heart. I was not sure I had a heart either until that day it attacked me.

What my heart had against me to attack me like that I still have not figured out.

Two years later, I have to go in for some tests, including a stress test.

The date was set for my test, and I wasn't supposed to drive myself because of the procedure, so The Gracious Mistress of the Parsonage drove me to my appointment in her Sissy Van.

That alone was a stress test. Just riding in that Sissy Van prepared me for my stress test, and I don't believe the doctor could do anything more stressful.

I went to the cardiac place and prepared for the procedure that would last more than an hour.

The first level of stress, which I considered the most severe level, I was not allowed to have any coffee for 12 hours before the test. I don't know about you, but I live on my morning coffee.

"You do know," I said to my doctor, "that without my coffee, I will be a mess?"

"That's all right, I've dealt with many people like that, and I plan to strap you down, and I will have a needle in my hand that I'm sure will direct your attention from your caffeine."

I was then escorted into a room with a nurse who told me I needed to remove my shirt and T-shirt so she could prep me.

I was nervous and told her, "That will cost you one dollar."

"What are you talking about?"

Looking at her seriously, I said, "I do not strip without getting paid."

It was then that my real stress test began. Nurses don't have a sense of humor.

I very cautiously removed my shirt and T-shirt and sat in the chair, and she came over and put all kinds of tabs on my chest. According to her, these tabs will be hooked up to lines that go to The Machine that will begin the test of my heart.

Getting all those tabs stuck on my chest in the right place took her a while.

"You don't plan to electrocute me, do you?"

She looked at me with a sinister grin and said, "Time will tell."

Now my stress went up another notch.

This was just the beginning. According to the schedule, I had at least another 45 minutes under some machine that would be doing another level of stress testing.

I was escorted back to the room where this would occur and introduced to two young guys who would set me on this machine.

"I'm going to give you a shot of some medicine, and you might feel a little dizzy or lightheaded. Don't worry. It's part of the process."

That sure was easy for him to say he didn't have to go through all this nonsense.

"Just relax. You might hear noises, see things, lights, and so forth, but you're okay; everything is under control."

I love it when a plan comes together, but this wasn't part of it.

I was put on the table, and then all of these cords were attached to the tabs on my chest. I was getting ready to go through that tunnel that was just behind me.

"You're going to be all right, and we have everything under control. Just relax, and maybe you even want to take a nap."

Right. I want to nap when somebody has hooked me up to cords I'm not sure what will happen. It's not that I don't trust doctors; I just don't trust doctors.

For the next 45 minutes, I was going through this machine, and I heard noises, saw flashes of light, and heard someone on the outside say, "Just breathe normally, and you might even just want to take a nap."

Then the stress test was over, and I could put on my shirt and T-shirt. They said everything went through just fine, and the doctor would get to me sometime next week with the results. I was then ushered to the outside, where The Gracious Mistress of the Parsonage was waiting to take me home, which was the last level of my stress test.

As I walked out, a lot of people in the lobby area were waiting for their doctor's appointments. As I walked out, everybody looked at me, which brought me to another level of stress.

Feeling slightly dizzy, I looked back at them, then pointed both hands to my face and said, "I've just had a facelift. How does it look."

For some reason, all the air was sucked out of the lobby, and even a couple laughed. Someone looked at my wife and said, "Is that your husband?" She smiled and ushered me out of the room to the waiting Sissy Van.

Stress can be very stressful; at least, that's my experience.

I couldn't help but think of a verse of Scripture. "Humble yourselves therefore under the mighty hand of God, that he may exalt you in due time: Casting all your care upon him; for he careth for you" (1 Peter 5:6-7).

I can try to handle everything on my own, or I can cast all my care upon the Lord. The choice is mine.

If Only I Had It My Way

Every once in a while, I have a little thought giggling in my brain to the effect that if only I had it my way. I don't have it often, but I try to take it seriously when I do.

My personal history is that it turns out to be a disaster whenever I have everything my way. And, boy, have I had disasters in my life.

I often think of Frank Sinatra's song, "I Did It My Way." For the life of me, I do not know what that is all about. Maybe it worked for him, but it hasn't worked for me, at least not yet. If I did everything my way, I'm sure I would be locked up in jail or an insane asylum by now. I'm not sure which is worse.

Regarding this, The Gracious Mistress of the Parsonage has several PhDs in "Doing It My Way." If I were smart and not saying I am, I would let her always have it her way.

There is only one place I can have anything my way: my Personal Interior Castle, my office. I sit at my desk; look at my computer, surrounded by thousands of books. In this "safe place," I can have it my way every day.

Occasionally, The Gracious Mistress of the Parsonage will come into my Interior Castle and say something to the effect, "Would you like me to do any organizing in here?"

I smile as best I can and respond, "You can organize in here if you permit me to go to your craft room and organize there." I then chuckle, knowing she would never permit me to enter her craft room, let alone organize anything.

Don't let this get out, but a couple of times when she's away, I sneak into her craft room and move things around so she can't find them when she needs them. When she returns, she will go into her craft room, and I will stand outside to listen and hear her say something to the effect, "Now, where is that? I know it was right here when I left."

I have to be careful that, you know who, does not hear me chuckling.

She has her space to do her thing her way, and I have my space to do my thing my way, and the twain shall never entangle themselves.

One of my great pleasures is that when she does something her way, and it turns out to be wrong. I have to keep my laughter under control in those circumstances.

We often go across town for appointments, and when we do that, I allow her to take her Sissy Van, and I ride along strap in on the passenger side. Driving across town, she always decides which way to go.

Just recently, we had an appointment across town at some new location. We'd never been there before, so we had to be careful driving to that location.

When we got to a certain traffic light, I told her, "You need to turn right here on this street."

Looking at me, she said, "I'm driving, and so I know where I'm going. I don't need any information from you. Sit back and let me do it my way."

With that, she turned left, and I could hardly hold my laughter because I knew where that street would end up.

Looking at me, she said, "Why are you laughing?"

"I was just thinking of a joke."

"Oh, yeah. What was that joke?"

I looked at her, and in a moment, I said, "Why was six afraid of seven?"

"I don't know, why was six afraid of seven?"

"Because," I said, "seven, eight, nine."

"So," she graveled, "that was the joke you were thinking of?"

It wasn't, but I had to use something to cover up my laughter.

All I had to do was wait, and when we came to the end of this street, we would find out that we were at the wrong end of town. Oh, I love it when a plan comes together.

When she finally realized we were at the wrong end of town, she looked at me, "Don't you dare say what you're thinking."

Then she turned around and headed in the right direction.

My problem is that I caught her doing it her way, and it was the wrong way, and I can't exploit it. I have to pretend that it didn't happen. Oh, how I wish I could remind her of this mistake every time we are in the car.

Of course, I know if I do that, there will be heavy consequences on my side to deal with. Sometimes it's best to keep some things under lock and key. But I do confess there are times while she is driving that I think of that mistake, and I can only smile.

Later that day, I was reminded of what the apostle Paul said. "Let no man deceive himself. If any man among you seemeth to be wise in this world, let him become a fool, that he may be wise. For the wisdom of this world is foolishness with God. For it is written, He taketh the wise in their own craftiness" (1 Corinthians 3:18-19.

My craftiness has never done well for me. I choose to trust God in every situation that is before me. After all, He knows best.

Have Giggle Will Laugh

I have many problems in my life. I have yet to recognize all of my problems, but I'm sure I will soon.

That's why it's so great to be married to someone like The Gracious Mistress of the Parsonage. There is no problem she cannot fix, and I have many examples to prove it.

There is one problem she hasn't been able to fix. That is, I laugh too much. At least, according to her.

If something happens or someone says something, I will start to giggle, and I know that in a short time, I will be laughing. I know how to laugh better than anybody I know. Just ask The Gracious Mistress of the Parsonage.

Through the years, I have tried to moderate it. I don't want to laugh at everything even though there is a giggle inside of me. Most people don't think everything is funny, while I, on the other side, can't think of anything that isn't funny.

Someone may tell me something or say something unwittingly, and I begin to giggle. I know when that starts I have no control over my giggle-itis. The only cure I have found for giggle-itis is laughter.

Someone may be telling a very serious story about their life, and I hear it wrong and think they are saying something altogether different, and it kicks in my giggle-itis.

It wouldn't be so bad if I could control it when it happens, but as history has proven, I cannot.

I do try to keep some things serious. I must confess, however, that changes from day to day. What is serious today may not be serious tomorrow, and I am the last one to know how to control that.

I've often discussed this with The Gracious Mistress of the Parsonage, and she has tried to counsel me in this area on how to control my laughter.

I try to explain to her that it is not so much the laughter as it is the giggle. If I could control my giggles, I wouldn't have any problem with laughter. She doesn't get it and laughs at me.

You must agree, there are many things in this world that are funny. And I do not believe we should overlook or ignore those situations.

Last week I was standing in line at the post office, and at the counter was a very nice older lady. She was paying for some postage and gave the cashier a $50 bill. Then the cashier, preparing to give her money back, said something strange. He said, "Mam, what denomination would you like?"

I hadn't heard that in a long time and was anxious to hear how the lady would respond.

She looked at the cashier with a very serious look and said, "Sir, I'm a Baptist, so give it to me in Baptist denomination."

Little did I know she was not joking, but I laughed at her, trying to conceal it.

The cashier stared at her, not knowing what to do. I'm not sure what money he gave her because I was laughing too much on the inside.

It's so hard for me to laugh on the inside and keep it from getting on the outside. What is inside eventually comes outside. I was laughing about that for the rest of the day. And still, when I think of it, I chuckle on the inside.

Just the other day, The Gracious Mistress of the Parsonage came and informed me that she would be gone for the day, thrift store shopping with her daughters. Looking at me, she seriously said, "Can you get your own lunch today while I'm gone?"

That tripped the giggle button inside for some reason, and my giggle-itis had kicked in.

Looking at her while giggling, I said, "Don't worry. I'll clean the refrigerator out by the time you get home."

Then I started laughing almost uncontrollably. She, on the other hand, looked at me with her infamous scowl and said, without laughing, "I don't think so."

I could not stop laughing as she walked out the front door. Several hours later, I was still laughing, and went and looked in the refrigerator to see how much work I had on hand.

When I opened the refrigerator door, I immediately stopped laughing. There at the front was a bowl of broccoli. I know she did that on purpose, and it cured my giggle-itis for a moment. I had to devise a plan for that broccoli to make me laugh and her scowl. Now the giggle-itis is beginning to turn on.

I think a bowl of Apple Fritters would be an excellent replacement. This is one of the few items that will make the Gracious Mistress of the Parsonage scowl. To see that scowl will be worth all I can offer at this time.

Just the thought of that began a giggle inside of me. Thinking more of this it developed into laughter. I just can't wait to get even.

While I was laughing, I thought of one my favorite Bible verses. "All the days of the afflicted are evil: but he that is of a merry heart hath a continual feast" (Proverbs 15:15).

When I think of broccoli I have evil feelings, but the Apple Fritter thought brings a lot of merriment to me.

Then I remembered, "A merry heart doeth good like a medicine: but a broken spirit drieth the bones."

Oh, Memory, How I Miss Thee

Driving home from a luncheon with friends, The Gracious Mistress of the Parsonage asked me a stunning question.

She is a specialist regarding questions I can't answer. I am trying to evade her questions and have been very good up until now.

"Did that story you told really happened?" She glanced at me with one of her quizzical looks.

Because I told several stories at lunchtime, I was wondering which one she was referring to. To the best of my knowledge, everything I say is true. Of course, people have different views of truth.

"Which story are you referring to, my dear?"

My plan has always been to deflect the attention away from the real question.

"You know. The one about the chicken attacking you."

Since I told quite a few stories, I couldn't remember that one exactly. My memory has a problem with really staying focused. I can tell one story one time and tell it again, and it is pretty different. If you heard both, you would know they were the same story.

It's not that I lie. I have a creative attitude and imagination with the stories I tell.

It's not the story I'm telling but rather the point I'm trying to convey.

"Well, my dear, if I told it, it must true because I do not lie except when I go to bed." But I smiled at her and nodded in a very affirmative way.

She didn't think that was funny and said so.

"Well," she said very seriously, "I've heard you tell that story at least six times and each time it's different. What do you have to say about that?"

Looking at her rather soberly, I said, "The only thing I can think of is that they were six different stories."

That is one of the astounding things about memory. If it's my memory, I should be able to tell it how I want to. After all, I can't remember back that far in my life. And, to tell the truth, it may not have happened at all. Who knows?

That is why if I tell any story, it is one before I met The Gracious Mistress of the Parsonage. All during our marriage, she has been very faithful in correcting the stories I tell while I'm telling them. At least those stories that happened while we were together.

That is the challenge I have just about every day of my life. The Gracious Mistress of the Parsonage has a flawless memory. Don't let her know I said this, but I suspect she remembers things that never happened. But with my flawed memory, there's no way I could correct that.

She knows everything that has ever happened since the day we first met. If only I had half of her memory skills. [Sigh!]

I learned this long ago, so if I tell a story, it was before I met Miss Know-It-All. Then, I can tell it according to my memory, which is somewhat flawed.

One of the blessings of a flawed memory is that I can tell a story that happened way back half a dozen times, and nobody would know it. Most of the time, I don't know it.

A long time ago, I accepted that I should not try to correct a story whenever she tells it.

Once, and only once, I thought I would agitate her, and as she told a story, I would correct it.

"No, my dear, it wasn't on a Tuesday, it was on a Friday."

On and on I went until I could see behind those beautiful eyes of her and growing agitation; that was a warning sign for me to SHUT UP. And UP, I SHUT.

On our way home that time, we had a long discussion. It was not a discussion; it was a monologue of what she thought about me correcting her when she was absolutely right about everything.

Common sense told me not to do that again. I think about it occasionally and can't help but chuckle. I want to do that one more time just before my funeral.

If I had her impeccable memory, my life would be so dull. I often change the memories that I do remember because nobody would know the difference, and I'm having fun.

Long ago, I stopped telling stories after I met The Gracious Mistress of the Parsonage because one slip up there will have a lifetime consequence.

I was sitting in my easy-chair with a hot cup of Joe reflecting on these things. I thought of what Solomon said about memory. "Blessings are upon the head of the just: but violence covereth the mouth of the wicked. The memory of the just is blessed: but the name of the wicked shall rot" (Proverbs 10:6-7).

Then I was reminded of what Peter said. "For he that will love life, and see good days, let him refrain his tongue from evil, and his lips that they speak no guile:

Let him eschew evil, and do good; let him seek peace, and ensue it" (1 Peter 3:10-11).

Memory can be a tricky thing for many, especially me. I'm trying to process Peter's warning here to "refrain my tongue from evil, and my lips that they speak no guile." If I'm honest with myself I must be honest with everyone else. Also what Solomon said, "The memory of the just is blessed" is important.

How to Get to Heaven

First the bad news

Because we have sinned we are born separated from God. Without intervention, we are ineligible for Heaven. This applies to the entire human race. You are not alone.

Romans 3:23 says, "For all have sinned, and come short of the glory of God;"
Romans 3:10 says, "As it is written, There is none righteous, no, not one:"
Romans 6:23a "For the wages of sin is death;"
Revelation 21:8 "But the fearful, and unbelieving, and the abominable, and murderers, and whoremongers, and sorcerers, and idolaters, and all liars, shall have their part in the lake which burneth with fire and brimstone:"
There is no amount of good works we can do to save ourselves from being eternally separated from God.

Ephesians 2:8-9 says, "For by grace are ye saved through faith; and that not of yourselves: it is the gift of God: Not of works, lest any man should boast."
To be separated from God forever, simply do nothing. To ignore or reject God's son is the only sin that can keep a person out of Heaven and the only alternative to Heaven is eternal torment in the Lake of Fire (Revelation 20:15, 2 Thes. 1:7-9).

John 3:18 "He that believeth on him is not condemned: but he that believeth not is condemned already, because he hath not believed in the name of the only begotten Son of God."

But there is good news!

There is a simple and free way to be reconciled with God made possible by God's only son Jesus. A blood sacrifice was needed to pay for your sins and Jesus was sent to become that sacrifice. He was nailed to a Roman cross to shed His blood in payment for your sin. Then three days after His death, He rose from the dead, validating once and for all His qualification to be our only Savior.

Placing your complete trust in Jesus' death, burial and resurrection is God's one and only means of reaching Heaven.

Jesus said (John 14:6), "I am the Way, the Truth, and the Life:, no man cometh unto the Father, but by me."

John 3:16 & 17 are clear. "For God so loved the world, that he gave his only begotten Son, that whosoever believeth in him should not perish, but have everlasting life. For God sent not his Son into the world to condemn the world; but that the world through him might be saved."

The Bible clearly tells us how to be saved:

Romans 10:9-10 "That if thou shalt confess with thy mouth the Lord Jesus, and shalt believe in thine heart that God hath raised him from the dead, thou shalt be saved. For with the heart man believeth unto

righteousness; and with the mouth confession is made unto salvation."
This is a free gift from God because He loves you.

Romans 6:23b "but the gift of God is eternal life through Jesus Christ our Lord."
Romans 10:13 "Whosoever shall call upon the name of the Lord shall be saved."

Are you ready to believe right now? If so, simply tell God what he asked you to confess. You might use a prayer similar to this one:

"God, I admit to you that I am a sinner and I know I cannot do anything to earn my way to Heaven. I truly believe that Jesus died on the cross, was buried and rose from the grave. I put my faith in His sacrifice to pay for my sin in full."

Contact us if you have prayed this prayer – jamessnyder51@Gmail.com